DISCARDED

THIS WE BELIEVE

Developmentally Responsive
Middle Level Schools

NATIONAL MIDDLE SCHOOL ASSOCIATION IS DEDICATED TO IMPROVING THE EDUCATIONAL EXPERIENCES OF YOUNG ADOLESCENTS BY PROVIDING VISION, KNOWLEDGE, AND RESOURCES TO ALL WHO SERVE THEM IN ORDER TO DEVELOP HEALTHY, PRODUCTIVE, AND ETHICAL CITIZENS.

THIS WE BELIEVE

Developmentally Responsive Middle Level Schools

A Position Paper of
NATIONAL MIDDLE SCHOOL ASSOCIATION

National Middle School Association
Columbus, Ohio

National Middle School Association
2600 Corporate Exchange Drive, Suite 370
NMSA Columbus, Ohio 43231

In light of relevant research, the cumulative experiences of thousands of middle school practitioners, and the vast societal changes that have occurred over the last decade, NMSA's Board of Trustees decided it was time to revisit its basic position paper, *This We Believe*. The Association applied to the Program for Student Achievement at the Edna McConnell Clark Foundation for a grant to assist in convening a committee to complete this task. NMSA appreciates the support received from the Edna McConnell Clark Foundation which allowed us to move forward with the development of this important position paper.

Likewise, the Association is indebted to the committee members listed on page 2 for their commitment to this undertaking. Their shared vision and practical understandings of a developmentally responsive middle school are inherent in this document. A subcommittee comprised of Gordon Vars, Ross Burkhardt, and John Lounsbury played an important role in the final crafting of the document. As editor, John Lounsbury deserves special recognition for his dedication, wisdom, and long hours spent molding the writings of committee members to bring this document to life. His involvement has been crucial to the success of this project.

Sue Swaim, Executive Director
National Middle School Association

Copyright© 1995, 3rd printing, April 1996
National Middle School Association

All rights reserved. No part of this publication may be reproduced or transmitted in any form or by any means without permission in writing from the publisher except in the case of brief quotations embodied in reviews or articles.

ISBN: 1-56090-105-5

Introduction

T he history of middle level or intermediate education now spans almost a century. In the early days of the junior high school movement, 1910-1925, several widely recognized position statements set forth the goals and responsibilities of this new American institution. Then in 1947 the six functions of the junior high school proposed by Gruhn and Douglass became the standard as efforts were made to revitalize that institution. However, following the introduction of the middle school in the 1960s with its advocacy of a 5-8 or 6-8 grade configuration, no single comprehensive statement appeared that seemed to crystallize the educational beliefs inherent in this emerging educational reform effort.

Recognizing the need for clarification and direction, John Swaim, the 1980 president of National Middle School Association, appointed a committee to prepare a position paper. That committee was chaired by Alfred A. Arth and included William Alexander, Charles Cherry, Donald Eichhorn, Conrad Toepfer, and Gordon Vars. After a period of many months and numerous drafts, a preliminary paper was submitted to John Lounsbury for refinement, editing, and publication. The final Board-approved document, *This We Believe*, was published in 1982.

Since its initial release, this position paper has had a far-reaching impact on middle level education. During the past 15 years it has been the most widely cited statement about the education of young adolescents. The 1982 issue of the document was reprinted seven times to meet the demand for its content. In 1992 the paper was reissued in a fresh format and subsequently had to be reprinted five times.

This We Believe has more than fulfilled our need for professional guidelines, and it will forever hold a place of honor and importance in the literature of middle level education. However, developments in education and in the practice of middle level education in particular have been so extensive since its release that the Association recognized the need to assemble a group to revisit that position paper. The document you hold in your hands is not just a revision, but a *re-vision* of middle level education that more fully expresses the Association's beliefs as we approach the twenty-first century.

Committee members charged with this responsibility were: John Arnold, Sherrel Bergmann, Barbara Brodhagen, Ross Burkhardt, Maria Garza-Lubeck, John Lounsbury, Marion Payne, Chris Stevenson, Sue Swaim, and Gordon Vars.

This statement is the result of that committee's intensive discussions, numerous drafts, suggestions received from members of the Board of Trustees and many other active middle level educators, and line by line refinements by a subcommittee. Like its predecessor, this position statement is not presumed to be all-inclusive or definitive, nor does it offer a specific blueprint for the "ideal" middle level school. The many specific topics identified in this paper are addressed in more detail through other Association publications and activities. This document, however, calls attention to essentials of both philosophy and practice. Thoughtful middle level educators will know best what needs to be done to apply these principles in their own communities.

This position paper was unanimously approved by NMSA's Board of Trustees in September 1995 and is offered to the profession and the public as a guide to assist in achieving developmentally responsive educational programs for young adolescents.

The Rationale for Middle Level Schools

The overarching purpose of all schooling in our society is to help students become good citizens, lifelong learners, and healthy, caring, ethical, and intellectually reflective individuals. The skills, knowledge, and personal competence that students acquire in school should enable them to be successful now and in the future. Middle level education is the segment of schooling that encompasses early adolescence, the stage of life between the ages of 10 and 15. In order to be developmentally responsive, middle level schools must be grounded in the diverse characteristics and needs of these young people. It is this concept that lies at the heart of middle level education. While grade configuration may be a consideration, the nature of the program provided for young adolescents, wherever they are housed, is the crucial factor.

Contemporary society presents remarkably different challenges from those that educators faced a few decades ago. While the traditional school functions of transmitting our heritage, teaching the tools of scholarship and the workplace, and promoting democratic citizenship remain valid, many practices of the past are no longer appropriate for the youth of today or the society in which they live. Educators therefore seek to provide schools that are joyful places where learning and learners are celebrated.

Young Adolescents

Young people undergo more rapid and profound personal changes during the years between 10 and 15 than at any other period of their lives. Although growth in infancy is also very extensive, infants are not the conscious witnesses of their development as are young adolescents. These developmental processes, while natural and necessary, often constitute challenges for youngsters as well as for their teachers, parents, and others entrusted with responsibility for their healthy development and education. However, tidy generalizations about youth are risky. Early adolescence is a period of tremendous variability among youngsters of the same gender and chronological age. Dissimilar rates of growth are common in all areas of development – intellectual, physical, social, emotional, and moral. Changes occur irregularly; no two young adolescents enter puberty at the same time or progress at the same rate. Individual differences proliferate, making dubious such assumptions as "All 7th graders are ..." It also is important to recognize that these areas of development are inexorably intertwined. With young adolescents, the achievement of academic success, for example, is highly dependent upon their other developmental needs being met.

Changes in patterns of thinking and learning become evident in students' ideas about the way things are and how they function. These shifts may be seen in questions they pose to each other and to trusted adults, in reflections about personal experiences, in their critiques of moral issues, and through their perceptions of stories, images, and humor. Young adolescents reveal growing capacity for conceptualization, for considering more than a single idea at a time, and for planning steps to carry out their own learning. Such evidence heralds growth toward more mature and abstract ways of thinking. Students benefit from learning systematic approaches to creative thinking and problem solving. However, because cognitive growth occurs gradually, most middle level students require ongoing concrete, experiential learning in order to develop intellectually.

These years also are characterized by surges of physical growth and accelerated movement toward reproductive maturity. Hormonal shifts trigger physical transformations such as: redistribution of body fat; weight and height increases; abrupt growth of bones and muscles; and changes in voice, hair, and complexion. In general, physical maturational processes commence earlier for girls than boys. Genital development prompts new physical, emotional, and social concerns for both sexes. Early or late physical maturation affects self-perception as well as status with peers and adults.

Concerns about appearance and body image usually generate heightened interest in personal grooming among young adolescents; yet, their health practices are often inappropriate, especially in relationship to diets needed to meet the nutritional needs of changing bodies. Too many youngsters begin experimenting with sex, and with tobacco, alcohol, and other harmful drugs, all of which pose serious threats to personal health. Rapid physical changes combined with the multiple hazards of contemporary life make this a crucial period for healthy personal growth and development.

One consuming aspect of young adolescent development is the search for personal identity. Young adolescents form their sense of self in large part from the interactions they have with significant peers and adults. Sensitive, knowledgeable adults recognize the importance of support and advocacy for those adolescents who are striving to establish themselves in positive, productive ways.

Parents and other family members almost always retain primary authority and continue as the source of basic values for children. However, young people's desire for peer acceptance and the need to belong to particular social groups are often intense, sometimes effecting transfers of allegiance from adults to peers. Issues of right or wrong, good or bad, appropriate or inappropriate may be influenced by the assertions or actions of other young adolescents. Parents, school authorities, and others should see this behavior as part of a young adolescent's striving for independence and should take care to keep lines of communication open.

The effects of societal forces upon moral development are of particular concern during early adolescence. Most young adolescents make wise life choices, but making those choices has become difficult in a world in which violence and greed are all too prevalent. Young people are confronted with conflicting messages about sexuality and appropriate behavior, and too often their schools shy away from such issues. Developmentally responsive middle schools, however, promote programs that actively assist young people in formulating the moral principles upon which they may ground their lives. This crucial guidance, of course, must be done with sensitivity and consideration of family and community expectations.

The Changing Society

The many transitions individuals undergo during adolescence would make growing up difficult enough in an unchanging culture. However, cultures today are evolving rapidly, and virtually every aspect of life has changed except for our children's innate developmental needs. Although children may mature physically more rapidly today, they still confront the same developmental hurdles as did previous generations.

The second half of the twentieth century brought unprecedented change to modern life, especially to male and female roles, family structures and traditions, influences of electronic and print media, and the increasingly diverse and multicultural nature of communities. Although modern life is richer in many ways, the roles of youth have become rather ambiguous, and young adolescents have few opportunities for meaningful service. They need supportive adult guidance and advocacy more than ever as they struggle to maintain the hope and optimism that have typically characterized youth.

Family structure is being redefined. Nuclear and extended families once provided clear roles, expectations, and responsibilities. Today nuclear families are less common, and more children than ever before are growing up without positive adult role models, particularly fathers. In addition, many children and youth simply lack adequate supervision – an unhealthy situation in an environment rife with temptations. Teachers and administrators are concerned that many children lack basic social skills and exhibit an indifference toward learning.

The economy also directly affects adolescents. A substantial number of young people have considerable disposable income and are a major target of marketing campaigns. Advertising strategies aimed at youth are often manipulative. Much of the entertainment in which young adolescents participate fosters superficial values, depicts gender roles inappropriately, and promotes a passive life-style. In addition, negative influences such as poverty, racism, sexism, crime, drugs, and child abuse confront young adolescents. The education of our youth, therefore, requires school and community programs that will cultivate responsible, moral decision makers and enlightened consumers.

A full understanding of the unique nature and needs of young adolescents makes clear many aspects of what ought to be characteristic of an educational program for 10-15 year olds. Guidelines for selecting educational goals, curriculum content, and instructional processes grow out of an awareness of this distinctive developmental age group.[1]

When coupled with an equally full understanding of the cultural context in which youth grow to maturity, educators have the essential foundation for making wise decisions about educational programs. National Middle School Association, fully aware of the fact that the experiences youth undergo during these formative years have lifelong influence, has sought to reconceptualize developmentally responsive middle level schools. Such schools will promote the growth of young adolescents as scholars, democratic citizens, and increasingly competent, self-sufficient young people who are optimistic about their future.

In the remainder of this document, the Association seeks to clarify a vision that can guide the decisions of those responsible for determining young adolescent educational programs, regardless of the particular school building in which they are located.

First, six general characteristics are identified. These are conditions that should be in place in order to make the most appropriate program decisions. When these are operational, schools are in the best position to make suitable provisions for an educational program that truly reflects student and societal needs. The paper then identifies and describes six major areas or program components. Taken together, these twelve characteristics delineate a vision of what developmentally responsive middle schools could be and should be.

---

[1] As a supplement to the descriptions provided in the rationale, a comprehensive listing of the characteristics of young adolescents in five categories is provided on pages 35-40.

National Middle School Association believes:

DEVELOPMENTALLY RESPONSIVE MIDDLE LEVEL SCHOOLS ARE CHARACTERIZED BY:

Educators committed to young adolescents

A shared vision

High expectations for all

An adult advocate for every student

Family and community partnerships

A positive school climate

THEREFORE, DEVELOPMENTALLY RESPONSIVE MIDDLE LEVEL SCHOOLS PROVIDE:

Curriculum that is challenging, integrative, and exploratory

Varied teaching and learning approaches

Assessment and evaluation that promote learning

Flexible organizational structures

Programs and policies that foster health, wellness, and safety

Comprehensive guidance and support services

Developmentally responsive middle level schools are characterized by...

EDUCATORS COMMITTED TO YOUNG ADOLESCENTS

Effective middle level educators make a conscious choice to work with young adolescents. They understand the developmental uniqueness of young adolescents and are as knowledgeable about their students as they are about the subject matter they teach. Such middle level educators form learning partnerships with their students, demonstrating empathy while engaging them in significant academic learning experiences.

Middle level educators are advocates for all young adolescents. They enjoy being in their presence and understand the dynamics of an ever-changing youth culture. They recognize the value of interdisciplinary work and integrated learning and are able to make sound pedagogical decisions based on the needs, interests, and special abilities of their students. They are sensitive to individual differences and respond positively to the natural diversity present in middle level classrooms.

Middle level educators also serve as role models for their students. Whether they realize it or not, their behavior sends important messages to young adolescents that complement curriculum content. Educators serve their students well when they model inclusive, collaborative, and team-oriented approaches to learning.

When dedicated and knowledgeable middle level educators work in concert, they create exciting possibilities for all their students. By blending vision and commitment they make a positive difference in the lives of young adolescents. The clear challenge is to provide a rigorous and relevant education based on the developmental needs of young adolescent learners. We need educators committed to young adolescents who can meet that challenge.

Educators need specific preparation before they enter middle level classrooms and continuous professional development as they pursue their careers. Guidelines and exemplary programs for the preparation of middle level educators have been published by the National Middle School Association and others. State departments of education and institutions of higher learning have a responsibility to develop appropriate programs to assist school districts in providing ongoing professional development. School districts must take advantage of these opportunities in order to secure, motivate, and sustain effective middle level educators.

A Shared Vision

A developmentally responsive middle level school is guided by a vision. Research and practice over the past three decades provide middle level educators with a solid foundation that informs our vision of middle level education. Idealistic and uplifting, that vision should reflect the very best we can imagine about all the elements of schooling, including student achievement, student-teacher relationships, and community participation. It becomes the basis for a written mission statement supported by all stakeholders – students, teachers, administrators, families, board of education members, and others in the community. The mission statement should take into account the district philosophy and goals as well as relevant state guidelines. The collaborative process of developing a vision and a shared mission statement is critical to the long-term success of that school. When a mission statement becomes operational, middle level educators pursue appropriate practices for young adolescents and provide a challenging academic program. The vision and mission must be revisited on a regular basis as circumstances change and new research and practices emerge.

HIGH EXPECTATIONS FOR ALL

Educators in developmentally responsive middle level schools hold and act upon high expectations for all students, and the students themselves have expectations of success. Such confidence promotes positive attitudes and behaviors and serves as motivation for students to achieve; low expectations lead to alienation, discouragement, and lack of effort. As young adolescents are quick to sense, teachers convey their expectations by their own examples as well as by gestures, casual remarks, and overall attitudes.

Young adolescents are curious and concerned about themselves and their world rather than being rebellious and argumentative as they are often portrayed in the media. They want to contribute and need adults who believe in them and who can provide appropriate challenge, opportunity, and support.

Successful middle level schools are grounded in the understanding that young adolescents are capable of far more than adults often assume. For example, in recent years middle level students have drafted and lobbied successfully for legislation that saves a state billions of gallons of water annually; they have persuaded authorities in a major city to fingerprint children to help curb kidnapping and runaway problems; and they have developed and operated from their seventh grade classroom the largest animal refuge and rehabilitation shelter in the Midwest.

Effecting high academic achievement for all students is not simply a matter of "raising abstract standards." It means empowering students to learn, to become intellectually engaged, and to behave in keeping with responsible citizenship. It calls for them to develop initiative and responsibility so that they can become all they are capable of becoming. It requires adults to start where students are, understanding their individual needs, interests, and learning styles, then fashion a substantive curriculum and pace learning to meet individual levels of understanding. Expectations are translated into standards that are concrete, clearly written with examples, frequently revisited, and congruent with the school's mission.

In schools genuinely responsive to young adolescents, the teachers and administrators also hold high expectations for themselves and for one another. Adults as well as young people tend to live up to expectations. Where adults expect much of themselves, there is every likelihood that they will not be disappointed when they expect much of their students.

An Adult Advocate for Every Student

All adults in developmentally responsive middle level schools are advocates for young adolescents. In addition, each student has one adult who knows and cares for that individual and who supports that student's academic and personal development. This designated advocate or advisor must be a model of good character and be knowledgeable about both young adolescent development and middle level education.

Advocates or advisors are not counselors, but they can identify behavioral changes in students that need to be brought to the attention of counselors, administrators, teachers, parents, and others who can provide appropriate support. As the link between school and home, the advocate is the primary person at the school with whom the family makes contact when communicating about the child.

To facilitate advocacy for students, middle level schools use a variety of organizational arrangements such as advisory programs, homebase groups, and team-based mentorships. These efforts are augmented by comprehensive guidance and support services. The ideal school demonstrates a continuity of caring that extends over the student's entire middle level experience so that no student is neglected.

FAMILY AND COMMUNITY PARTNERSHIPS

Families and community members are important stakeholders in developmentally responsive middle level schools. Schools recognize and support families and community members as participants in school programs by encouraging their roles in supporting learning and honoring them as essential volunteers. Parents, families, and community members can enrich the curriculum and facilitate learning. The school takes the initiative in providing a wide variety of opportunities for parent and community involvement.

Since parents are the child's first teachers, effective schools support and assist parents and families in creating and sustaining positive home learning environments. Some parents become less involved when their children reach the middle level, while other families have had little involvement in their children's education from the beginning. But since school achievement is directly related to the degree of family support and involvement in the child's education, systematic, two-way communication with parents and families becomes especially critical. Regular school newsletters, student progress reports, parent-teacher conferences, telephone calls, and special bulletins are useful communication tools.

Middle level schools seek appropriate partnerships with businesses, social service agencies, and other organizations whose purposes are consistent with the school's mission. Students often become involved in apprenticeships, shadow studies, service learning projects, and other uses of the community as a learning site. Community members and school partners provide considerable assistance and expertise in the school-based instructional program as well.

In any partnership or venture, all parties must benefit and have mutually understood roles and expectations. The school-family-community relationship is no different. Schools should expect families and the community to take advantage of opportunities provided for involvement in support of education. Further, families should spend time sharing and engaging in their children's learning and modeling behaviors and skills essential for school success.

A Positive School Climate

The climate of a developmentally responsive middle level school is safe, inviting, and caring; it promotes a sense of community and encourages learning. A visitor walking into a middle level building immediately develops some first impressions. The cordial, pleasant tone of the staff and the way students greet and treat each other are revealing. Interactions among staff members and between students and staff reflect democracy and fairness. In a healthy school environment, human relationships are paramount, and all individuals are treated with dignity and respect. Students and adults recognize and accept one another's differences; curiosity, creativity, and diversity are celebrated. Issues of gender and equity are addressed with sensitivity and fairness. The climate encourages positive risk-taking, initiative, and the building of substantive relationships.

A good middle school is a healthy community composed of persons of differing ages, roles, and responsibilities. In many ways the school principal as an instructional leader is the key player in developing the positive school climate. The principal fosters open communication among all constituents, inviting them to collaborate in developing a shared vision for the school and building a successful educational program. Students and staff are empowered as they share in the decision-making process.

A clean, well-maintained physical plant is another indicator of a positive school climate. Student work is on display, the ambiance is student-centered, and it is clear that learning is the priority. Like young adolescents, the climate of a developmentally responsive middle level school requires constant nurturing.

Therefore, developmentally responsive middle level schools provide...

CURRICULUM THAT IS CHALLENGING, INTEGRATIVE, AND EXPLORATORY

Curriculum is the primary vehicle for achieving the goals and objectives of a school. To most, curriculum refers to the content and skills to be covered in courses. In developmentally responsive middle level schools, however, curriculum embraces every planned aspect of a school's educational program. It includes those specific classes designed to advance academic skills and knowledge as well as school-wide services such as guidance, clubs and interest groups, music and drama productions, student government, and sports. Although learning occurs in many unanticipated ways, curriculum is intentionally designed to accomplish a school's mission. Curriculum and procedures should be articulated with those of elementary and high schools, and there should be carefully planned orientation programs to help students make the transition from one institution to the next.

Middle level curriculum is distinguished by emphases that stem from the unique characteristics and needs of young adolescents. The curriculum of a developmentally responsive middle level school is challenging, integrative, and exploratory.

Challenging

Challenging curriculum actively engages young adolescents, marshalling their sustained interest and effort. It must address substantive issues and skills that are relevant; be geared to their levels of understanding; and enable them increasingly to assume control of their learning. Learning tasks must be perceived by the student as achievable, even if difficult.

Emphasis on important ideas and skills requires teachers to move well beyond "covering material." Using good judgment in consultation with students, they select ideas for in-depth study from a vast range of information and materials that are genuinely important and worth knowing. For these issues to come alive, values, assumptions, basic principles, and alternative points of view must be explored. Skills must be taught and learned in context, addressing "why" as well as "how." Focus is upon motivating students to be skilled as writers rather than just being able to write correctly.

Relevant curriculum involves students in activities that help them understand themselves and the world around them. It is rich in personal meaning. Teachers address students' own questions and concerns, which are then examined in a wider context. Making curriculum relevant thus does not mean limiting content solely to students' preexisting interests. Challenging curriculum creates new interests; it opens doors to new knowledge and opportunities; it "stretches" students.

Given the developmental diversity in any middle level classroom, gearing curriculum to students' levels of understanding is a daunting task. In addition to different rates of development and learning styles, varying cultural backgrounds and prior experience must be taken into account. Efforts to reduce tracking and to include students with special needs in regular classes increase the diversity even further. Adapting curriculum so as to challenge each and every student requires significant collaboration among regular and special education teachers, counselors, school social workers, parents, and the students themselves.

In essence, every student needs an individualized educational plan. Both content and methods must be individualized. As a first step, teachers can provide choices among learning opportunities, ranging from those that tax even the most gifted and talented students to those that enable the least capable to succeed with a reasonable expenditure of effort. Independent study, small group work, special interest courses, and apprenticeships are other means by which curriculum can challenge students through addressing individual needs.

Because of young adolescents' drive toward independence, curriculum that challenges must enable them increasingly to guide the course of their education. Consonant with their varying capacities to handle responsibility, students must be nurtured in making choices and decisions about curricular goals, content, methodology, activities, materials, and means of assessment. In addition, they should have opportunities for involvement in team governance which emphasizes student initiative and responsibility.

Integrative

Curriculum is integrative when it helps students make sense out of their life experiences. This requires curriculum that is itself coherent, that helps students connect school experiences to their daily lives outside the school, and that encourages them to reflect on the totality of their experiences. This goal may be accomplished in several ways.

Middle level schools can offer courses and units, taught either by individual teachers or by teams, that are designed specifically to integrate the formal school curriculum. In addition, all teachers can identify the connections among ideas and fields of knowledge, as well as how their teaching relates to the courses and student activities conducted by other school personnel. Reading, writing, critical thinking, and other skills should be taught and practiced wherever they apply, not just in isolation. Moreover, all teachers should explain how the content and skills they teach are applicable to the daily lives of their students. Journals, conferences, or other vehicles provide students with opportunities to reflect on their experiences, an essential step toward taking charge of their own lives and seeing life's interconnections. Reflection on experience also is a natural part of student self-evaluation.

Integration in all these dimensions is enhanced when the curriculum is focused on issues significant both to students and adults. Since real-life issues are by nature interdisciplinary, attention to them integrates the curriculum in natural ways. Intellectual, communication, social, physical, and technological skills are learned and applied in context. Critical thinking, decision-making, and creativity are enhanced when students examine appropriate problems and take steps to help solve them. In such cases, students produce or construct knowledge rather than simply act as consumers of knowledge.

Exploratory

The entire curriculum, not just certain courses or activities, should be exploratory. There are three earmarks of an exploratory curriculum. First, it enables students to discover their particular abilities, talents, interests, values, and preferences. This self-knowledge helps students to prepare for adult life, not only in terms of vocation, but also as family members and citizens. Second, all courses and activities are taught so as to reveal opportunities for making contributions to society. Finally, exploratory experiences acquaint students with enriching, healthy leisure-time pursuits, such as lifetime physical activities, involvement in the arts, and social service. Such a curriculum helps to develop young adolescents who will become well-rounded adults.

Developing curriculum is an important responsibility for all educators. They must cultivate the disposition and skills of scholarship and provide learning experiences that both draw from and integrate the disciplines. The rapid expansion of knowledge constitutes the ongoing and difficult task of selecting subject matter that is at the same time challenging, integrative, and exploratory. The responsibility of designing developmentally appropriate educational experiences for young adolescents is a challenge worthy of our best efforts.

VARIED TEACHING AND LEARNING APPROACHES

The distinctive developmental and learning characteristics of young adolescents provide the foundation for selecting teaching strategies, just as they do for designing curriculum. Teaching techniques should enhance and accommodate the diverse skills, abilities, and knowledge of young adolescents, cultivate multiple intelligences, and capitalize on students' individual learning styles. Students should acquire diverse ways of posing and solving questions and engage in learning activities wherein basic skills can be taught in functional contexts. New concepts should be built on the knowledge students already possess. Effective learning experiences capitalize on students' cultural, experiential, and personal backgrounds.

Since young adolescents learn best through engagement and interaction, learning strategies feature activities that provide hands-on experiences and actively involve youngsters in learning. While direct instruction is still important, varied approaches are needed, including experiments, demonstrations, opinion polls, simulations, and independent study.

Regular and special education teachers collaborate to design learning activities that provide appropriate challenges for all types of learners. There is emphasis on collaboration and cooperation, providing much-needed opportunities for peer interaction as well as increasing achievement. Varying forms of group work are used, depending on the purpose, with students at different times clustered randomly, by ability, by interest, or by other criteria.

Individual differences also are accommodated through numerous opportunities for student choice, both within the regular classroom and in electives and co-curricular programs that appeal to students with special talents or interests – intellectual, athletic, or artistic. School personnel consult with the families of students who have special needs in determining the best educational program for those students.

Instructional materials and resources are most worthwhile when they reflect multiple viewpoints and encourage young adolescents to explore new ideas. The community is a major resource, providing materials and personnel for in-class activities as well as being a site for learning experiences.

Technological resources should advance instruction whenever appropriate and possible. Educational technologies offer new pathways to learning, encourage the emergence of higher-order thinking skills, and enable teachers and students to interact with real world resources in unprecedented ways. Educators must have sufficient training to access information via these technologies. Students need to investigate both the positive and negative aspects of what it means to live in a technological society. Above all, newer learning technologies should be integrated into the curriculum; the computer and its cohorts serve as instructional tools for accessing information and enhancing learning.

ASSESSMENT AND EVALUATION
THAT PROMOTE LEARNING

Continuous, authentic, and appropriate assessment and evaluation are essential components of the learning process at any age level, providing information that students, teachers, and family members need to plan further learning.

Students should set personal standards and assess their progress in achieving both the knowledge and behavioral goals of an education. Learning activities ought to culminate in some form of sharing, demonstrating, publishing, displaying, or creating behavioral evidence that augments that obtained through more conventional testing. Assessment strategies are learning strategies as well as means of making evaluative judgments.

Although the words are often used interchangeably, assessment and evaluation are distinctly different. Assessment is the process of measuring a student's progress toward a goal or objective. Evaluation is the process of using data and standards to judge the quality of progress. Criteria for evaluation should be specified in advance and formulated with appropriate involvement of students and their parents or guardians. Assessment and evaluation ought to deal with both the processes and the products of learning and take into account student differences. Middle level students need to participate in all phases of assessment and evaluation, helping to set individual and group goals, identifying ways to measure progress, and evaluating their own accomplishments.

In addition to academic content and skills, assessment and evaluation should address other aspects of a student's growth such as critical thinking, curiosity, and other desired personal attributes. This requires a variety of assessment procedures, such as checklists and observation scales, in addition to traditional tests. Students can assemble portfolios and carry out demonstrations that reveal growth in many dimensions and categories.

In developmentally responsive middle level schools, assessment and evaluation procedures reflect the characteristics and uniqueness of young adolescents. Since early adolescence is a crucial period in establishing a clear self-concept and positive self-esteem, assessment and evaluation should emphasize individual progress rather than comparison with other students. The goal is to help students discover and understand their strengths, weaknesses, interests, values, and personalities. Student self-evaluation is an important means of developing a fair and realistic self-concept. Responsible middle level educators design assessment and evaluation activities that allow young men and young women equal opportunity when measuring academic progress.

Young adolescents' concern for peer approval is another reason to emphasize individualized evaluation and to minimize comparing students. Cooperative learning, with assessment based on both group and individual performance, capitalizes on this need and promotes both academic learning and the development of interpersonal skills. Occasional use of peer evaluation further demonstrates that teachers and students alike are involved in the assessment process.

All students who make reasonable effort should see their efforts rewarded. Emphasis should be on what the student has accomplished, not the failure to reach some arbitrary uniform standard. It also is important to help students and their families see how a student's performance corresponds with national or state norms. Such information is useful for planning careers and further education, yet it should not be the dominant concern during the middle level years.

Another characteristic of young adolescents, their desire for independence, often leads to breakdowns in communication with adults in the family. When the reporting of student progress is a joint venture among student, family, and school, that gap is bridged. Student-led conferences with teachers and family members are highly desirable and lead to continuous two-way communication between home and school. Various kinds of written reports from both students and teachers, plus telephone messages, are essential to keep home and school working together for the benefit of the young adolescent. A number or letter on a report card cannot adequately communicate a student's progress in school.

FLEXIBLE ORGANIZATIONAL STRUCTURES

Developmentally appropriate middle level schools are flexible in grouping, scheduling, and staffing. Large schools are subdivided into "houses" or "schools-within-a-school," each of which replicates on a smaller scale the same mix of grade levels, ethnic groups, and socioeconomic status that make up the school as a whole. Houses may be further subdivided into inter-disciplinary teams that build a sense of community and promote curriculum integration. Scheduling and staffing accommodate the need for teachers in all areas to interact with their colleagues whether or not they are formally assigned to a team.

In lieu of academic tracking, schools use enrichment programs, cooperative learning groups, and independent study to respond to the variety of student competencies, interests, and abilities. A block schedule permits teaching teams to vary the length of time in periods and also vary the size of class groups. In such a sched-ule two or three class groups, an entire grade level, or the whole student body can meet together when desirable. Daily common planning time for teams of teachers who instruct the same stu-dents is essential in order to coordinate their activities, integrate their instruction, and enhance their efforts to effect high academic achievement for all students. Bells are rarely needed since not all groups move to other classrooms at the same time.

Instruction may occur in many places other than the class-room, such as the cafetorium, the media center, or the school grounds. Students go into the community to use the resources found there, to learn responsible citizenship, and to provide mean-ingful service. Classroom furniture accommodates cooperative learning groups, student-to-student communication and discus-sions, learning centers, and other arrangements. Facilities are available for both team or grade meetings and for small group planning or rehearsals.

In exemplary middle level schools, teachers design and oper-ate much of the program, collaborate across teaching specialties, and share responsibility for literacy development, guidance/ad-vocacy, and student life. They make flexible use of time, space, staff, and grouping arrangements in order to match each student with the most appropriate selections from the many opportunities available.

PROGRAMS AND POLICIES THAT FOSTER HEALTH, WELLNESS, AND SAFETY

Developmentally responsive middle level schools provide abundant opportunities for students to achieve and maintain healthy minds and bodies and to understand their own growth. An emphasis on health, wellness, and safety permeates the entire school. The curriculum embraces a comprehensive program that includes daily physical education activities designed to improve students' cardiovascular fitness, coordination, agility, and strength. Lifelong physical activities such as movement, dance, and leisure-time sports are emphasized. Schools also recognize students for gains they make toward personal goals that are based on individual wellness profiles. Intramural and extracurricular activities that require physical participation are developmentally appropriate and comply with recognized national standards.

A comprehensive health and fitness program deals with such topics as nutrition, substance abuse, mental health, safety, peer mediation, sexual harassment, and health services. These areas provide opportunities for developing and practicing healthful decision-making, coping, and refusal skills which are reinforced elsewhere in the curriculum. Written policies undergird and direct the school's physical education, health, and wellness programs. Adults model good health habits and practices. Local health agencies collaborate with the school and with families in dealing with young adolescent health issues.

Schools actively promote a safe environment by developing school and community-wide initiatives that address risks and provide protective conditions through a home-school-community partnership. A school that fosters safety strives to build resiliency in young people by maintaining an environment in which peaceful and safe interactions are expected and are supported by written policies that help to assure consistent and fair practices. These policies are clearly communicated to students, teachers, families, and community members. A sense of school community is also developed by helping teachers and students manage anger, resolve conflicts peacefully, and prevent hateful or violent behaviors.

COMPREHENSIVE GUIDANCE AND SUPPORT SERVICES

Young adolescents live in an environment that presents them with many choices. Students bring events in their out-of-school lives to school. Developmentally responsive middle level schools, therefore, provide both teachers and specialized professionals who are readily available to offer the assistance many students need.

Teacher advocates and advisory programs provide ongoing assistance to help students successfully negotiate early adolescence. Homebase, advisory, and interdisciplinary team programs provide opportunities for advocates to meet regularly with their students individually and in small groups during the school day. Such programs are carefully designed to help students develop respect for self and others. They foster compassion, a workable set of values, and the skills of cooperation, decision-making, and goal-setting. The design of the advocacy program is based on the specific culture of the individual school and community and is developed to meet the needs of those particular students. Advocates receive ongoing staff development to help them fulfill this vital role.

There are occasions when students confront problems so serious that they require the more specialized services of counselors, health professionals, and social workers. All faculty are aware of appropriate referral services and procedures to follow when recommending students for specialized services.

School counselors support teachers in advocacy programs, demonstrate group activities, and offer one-on-one and small group guidance sessions for students as needed. They may sponsor and coordinate programs such as peer mediation and peer tutoring. They often share their expertise with teams and individual teachers and serve as resource persons in classroom activities. They also meet with parents, often in conjunction with teams or individual teachers.

School counselors coordinate the support services provided by the school system, ensuring the most efficient use of specialists such as school psychologists, social workers, and speech therapists. They see that the guidance services are articulated with those of the district's elementary and high schools.

A Call for Action

*T**his We Believe: Developmentally Responsive Middle Level Schools* is National Middle School Association's primary position paper. It is, as well, the Association's call for action. The Association encourages the use of this document as a framework to implement and sustain schools especially designed for young adolescents.

Educators, parents, and community members are urged to forge new and meaningful partnerships in order to transform *This We Believe* into a living document. It is time to launch those initiatives not yet begun, to strengthen those now underway, and for all stakeholders to re-dedicate themselves to the work needed to ensure the realization of these ideas and ideals.

The importance of achieving developmentally responsive middle level schools cannot be overemphasized. The nature of the educational programs young adolescents experience during this formative period of life will, in large measure, determine the future for all of us.

Characteristics of Young Adolescents

Y outh between the ages of 10 to 15 are characterized by their diversity as they move through the puberty growth cycle at varying times and rates. Yet as a group they reflect important developmental characteristics that have major implications for those agencies that seek to serve them.

In the area of **Intellectual Development**, young adolescents:

- Display a wide range of individual intellectual development

- Are in a transition period from concrete thinking to abstract thinking

- Are intensely curious and have a wide range of intellectual pursuits, few of which are sustained

- Prefer active over passive learning experiences

- Prefer interaction with peers during learning activities

- Respond positively to opportunities to participate in real life situations

This list is a revision and an expansion of the one originally prepared by the Maryland Task Force on the Middle Learning Years and published in 1989 by the Maryland State Department of Education in the report., *What Matters in the Middle Grades: Recommendations for Maryland Middle Grades Education.*

- Are often preoccupied with self

- Have a strong need for approval and may be easily discouraged

- Develop an increasingly better understanding of personal abilities

- Are inquisitive about adults, often challenging their authority, and always observing them

- May show disinterest in conventional academic subjects but are intellectually curious about the world and themselves

- Are developing a capacity to understand higher levels of humor

In the area of **Moral Development**, young adolescents:

- Are generally idealistic, desiring to make the world a better place and to become socially useful

- Are in transition from moral reasoning which focuses on "what's in it for me" to that which considers the feelings and rights of others

- Often show compassion for those who are downtrodden or suffering and have special concern for animals and the environmental problems that our world faces

- Are moving from acceptance of adult moral judgments to development of their own personal values; nevertheless, they tend to embrace values consonant with those of their parents

- Rely on parents and significant adults for advice when facing major decisions

- Increasingly assess moral matters in shades of grey as opposed to viewing them in black and white terms characteristic of younger children

- At times are quick to see flaws in others but slow to acknowledge their own faults

- Owing to their lack of experience are often impatient with the pace of change, underestimating the difficulties in making desired social changes

- Are capable of and value direct experience in participatory democracy

- Greatly need and are influenced by adult role models who will listen to them and affirm their moral consciousness and actions as being trustworthy role models

- Are increasingly aware of and concerned about inconsistencies between values exhibited by adults and the conditions they see in society

In the area of **Physical Development**, young adolescents:

- Experience rapid, irregular physical growth

- Undergo bodily changes that may cause awkward, uncoordinated movements

- Have varying maturity rates, with girls tending to mature one and one-half to two years earlier than boys

- May be at a disadvantage because of varied rates of maturity that may require the understanding of caring adults

- Experience restlessness and fatigue due to hormonal changes

- Need daily physical activity because of increased energy

- Develop sexual awareness that increases as secondary sex characteristics begin to appear

- Are concerned with bodily changes that accompany sexual maturation and changes resulting in an increase in nose size, protruding ears, long arms, and awkward posture

- Have preference for junk foods but need good nutrition

- Often lack physical fitness, with poor levels of endurance, strength, and flexibility

- Are physically vulnerable because they may adopt poor health habits or engage in risky experimentation with drugs and sex.

In the area of **Emotional/Psychological Development**, young adolescents:

- Experience mood swings often with peaks of intensity and unpredictability

- Need to release energy, often resulting in sudden, apparently meaningless outbursts of activity

- Seek to become increasingly independent, searching for adult identity and acceptance

- Are increasingly concerned about peer acceptance

- Tend to be self-conscious, lacking in self-esteem, and highly sensitive to personal criticism

- Exhibit intense concern about physical growth and maturity as profound physical changes occur

- Increasingly behave in ways associated with their sex as sex role identification strengthens

- Are concerned with many major societal issues as personal value systems develop

- Believe that personal problems, feelings, and experiences are unique to themselves

- Are psychologically vulnerable, because at no other stage in development are they more likely to encounter so many differences between themselves and others.

In the area of **Social Development**, young adolescents:

- Have a strong need to belong to a group, with peer approval becoming more important as adult approval decreases in importance

- In their search for self, model behavior after older, esteemed students or non-parent adults

- May exhibit immature behavior because their social skills frequently lag behind their mental and physical maturity

- Experiment with new slang and behaviors as they search for a social position within their group, often discarding these "new identities" at a later date

- Must adjust to the social acceptance of early maturing girls and the athletic successes of early maturing boys, especially if they themselves are maturing at a slower rate

- Are dependent on parental beliefs and values but seek to make their own decisions

- Are often intimidated and frightened by their first middle level school experience because of the large numbers of students and teachers and the size of the building

- Desire recognition for their efforts and achievements

- Like fads, especially those shunned by adults

- Often overreact to ridicule, embarrassment, and rejection

- Are socially vulnerable because, as they develop their beliefs, attitudes, and values, the influence of media and negative experiences with adults and peers may compromise their ideals and values.

NATIONAL MIDDLE SCHOOL ASSOCIATION

National Middle School Association was established in 1973 to serve as a voice for professionals and others interested in the education of young adolescents. The Association has grown rapidly and now enrolls members in all fifty states, the Canadian provinces, and dozens of foreign countries. In addition, fifty-three state, regional, and provincial middle school associations are official affiliates of NMSA.

NMSA is the only association dedicated exclusively to the education, development, and growth of young adolescents. Membership is open to all. While middle level teachers and administrators make up the bulk of the membership, central office personnel, college and university faculty, state department officials, other professionals, parents, and lay citizens are also actively involved and support our single mission – improving the educational experiences of 10 to15 year olds. This open membership with a limited focus is a particular strength of NMSA.

The Association provides a variety of services, conferences, and materials in fulfilling its mission. In addition to *Middle School Journal*, the movement's premier professional journal, the Association publishes *Research in Middle Level Education Quarterly*, a wealth of books and monographs, videos, a general newsletter, an urban education newspaper, and occasional papers. The Association's highly acclaimed annual conference, which has drawn over 10,000 registrants in recent years, is held in the fall.

For information about National Middle School Association and its many services contact the Headquarters at 2600 Corporate Exchange Drive, Suite 370, Columbus, Ohio 43231, TELEPHONE 800-528-NMSA, FAX 614-895-4750.